Behaviour Policy and Practice:
Self-Evaluation Pack for Schools

Published in 2001

ISBN 1 901485 29 3

Published by NASEN.
NASEN is a company limited by guarantee, registered in England and Wales.
Company No. 2674379.
NASEN is a registered charity. Charity No. 1007023.

Further copies of this book and details of NASEN's many other publications may be obtained from the Publications Department at its registered office:
NASEN House, 4/5 Amber Business Village, Amber Close, Amington, Tamworth, Staffs. B77 4RP.
Tel: 01827 311500; Fax: 01827 313005
Email: welcome@nasen.org.uk; Website: www.nasen.org.uk

Typeset in Times by J. C. Typesetting.
Printed in the United Kingdom by Stowes (Stoke-on-Trent).

Behaviour Policy and Practice: Self-Evaluation Pack for Schools

MANUAL

Contents

Preface

This publication is the result of an initiative begun in Kingston upon Hull. The Local Education Authority has a range of provision for pupils with behaviour difficulties including peripatetic support for schools, Pupil Referral Units and special school provision. The schools and LEA have been successful in keeping the number of exclusions relatively low. Even so, the perception remains widespread, as nationally, that more pupils are presenting ever more difficult behaviour.

Providers of behaviour support in the authority were brought together to consider the way forward. They believed that early intervention and prevention were the key – and that the focus for this should be mainstream school policy and practice. The critical question then was whether there could be agreement on exactly what constitutes good policy and practice. If there were a shared view that would be accepted as credible by schools, criteria could be developed by which this could be judged. Rather than adopting any particular approach being marketed, e.g. assertive discipline, a working party concentrated on the fundamental principles, as reflected in legislation, DfEE guidance and the OFSTED framework.

The working party began collating the recommended features of behaviour policies and practice and collated a summary of guidance. When the summary was translated into questions, the result provided the critical criteria for evaluation. In Kingston upon Hull, schools that satisfactorily fulfil the criteria are recognised by an accreditation scheme. The scheme thereby encourages a positive approach to developing good whole school behaviour policies, rather than the traditional problem solving model of finding and remedying weaknesses. It also provides independent recognition for schools that are managing behaviour well.

The Kingston upon Hull Behaviour Accreditation Scheme has been in place since 1997, and was recently complimented in the authority's OFSTED inspection.

Many people have been involved in its development, including support service staff, head teachers, advisers and senior officers. Although initially targeting the primary sector, the criteria questionnaire has also been used successfully by secondary and special schools. When the scheme needed to be thoroughly reviewed in the light of new Government legislation and advice, it seemed timely to enable all schools to benefit through its broader publication.

Acknowledgements

I would like to acknowledge the many people in Kingston upon Hull Learning Services who contributed to an original version of this publication – teachers, officers, advisers, heads and in particular the working party in the Special Educational Needs Support Service.

Alec Williams of the NASEN Publications Sub-Committee recognised the potential of an updated and revised version being made available to all schools through publication. He has freely given time and patient enthusiasm to advise on successive drafts and his personal support has been invaluable.

Sue Young
(Behaviour Accreditation Scheme Coordinator, Kingston upon Hull Learning Services)

How to use the self-evaluation pack

Aims of the pack

Behaviour Policy and Practice: Self-Evaluation Pack for Schools enables schools to record their reviews of behaviour policy and practice against comprehensive evaluation criteria. It can be used by individual schools, or by advisers, educational psychologists or behaviour support staff when assisting schools in this endeavour. It also provides the means to document the development of a school's behaviour policy and practice over time, against fixed criteria.

There are two separate parts to the pack:

1) this MANUAL which needs to be read before completing the Schedule and also consulted throughout the evaluation process;
2) the SCHEDULE and a summary development plan which are printed as a separate booklet for ease of use. These are for recording the evaluation and the resulting action to be taken.

Reasons to review the behaviour policy

All schools need to review their behaviour policy from time to time. At the present time in particular, recent changes in legislation with associated DfEE circulars and the new OFSTED Framework for Inspection and Guidance require attention. Action needs to be taken to incorporate the changes they have brought into the school behaviour policy.

Inevitably, schools often wait until there are concerns about behaviour before a review of policy is given priority. These concerns may arise as a result of a perception that there is a general deterioration in standards of behaviour in the school or there may be a particularly difficult group of pupils attracting attention. However, there are several advantages to reviewing behaviour policy and practice at a time other than crisis:

- A behaviour policy is as much about encouraging positive qualities and values as preventing difficult behaviour.
- Only through continuous development can high standards be maintained.
- The ethos of a school is always capable of further improvement.
- Identifying and articulating strengths and qualities in a school enhances them and ensures their continuance.

No two schools have the same behaviour policy. Even if a structured approach such as assertive discipline has been used to develop the policy, all schools will differ in detail so that the policy reflects their own special ethos. This is entirely appropriate and to be encouraged. Every school needs to command ownership of its behaviour policy so that the school community is actively committed to it and participates in its continuous development. However, there are certain constraints on that freedom. The Manual makes clear the parameters within which any behaviour policy needs to operate.

Legislation

Policies and practice on the behaviour policy itself, attendance, exclusions and home-school agreements have all been affected by recent legislation, particularly by the School Standards and Framework Act 1998. The Summary of Guidance in this Manual explains the legal requirements, with extracts and appropriate references. The Schedule provides the check that all is in place.

DfEE guidance

Some DfEE publications, including the circulars, provide advice on the law that goes beyond interpretation. Some is statutory, that is schools are required to 'have regard to' the advice e.g. *Home-School Agreements: Guidance for schools*. In practice, all DfEE circulars provide guidelines that schools should follow as the basis of good practice. Other DfEE publications, such as research reports, may be influential but are not intended to be prescriptive. They provide useful background information. All statutory guidance is referred to in the Summary of Guidance in the Manual and checked in the Schedule. Other DfEE sources are used selectively.

OFSTED

An OFSTED inspection pays particular attention to policy and practice in terms of outcomes and takes a broad view of how schools influence and promote good behaviour. As a result, pupil behaviour is explicitly considered across four different aspects of the new inspection framework:

- *How high are standards?*
  Part 1: The Schools' Results and Achievements
  Part 2: Pupils' Attitudes, Values and Personal Development
- *How well are pupils taught?*
- *How good are the curricular and other opportunities offered to pupils?*
- *How well does the school care for its pupils?*

The criteria on which judgements are based during an OFSTED inspection are detailed in OFSTED's *Inspecting Schools: The Framework* and guidance on the criteria is detailed in the Handbooks. The Summary of Guidance in the Manual draws attention to the main criteria and the Schedule provides the check. In fact, the OFSTED handbooks themselves suggest that their criteria could be used in just this way[1].

Aspects of the behaviour policy

To make the evaluation process manageable it is divided into ten corresponding sections, one for each aspect, in the Manual, Schedule and development plan. This is necessarily an uneasy division and the different aspects are in fact co-dependent. They are self-explanatory but the three aspects below have particular issues that need further clarification.

Attendance

The issue of attendance, or more precisely unauthorised absence, has been brought to the fore in recent years and occupies a central place in the recent DfEE Circular 10/99 *Social Inclusion: Pupil Support* on behaviour. Non-attendance can be seen in some cases as a response to school similar to disruptive behaviour, a sign of disaffection. The Social Exclusion Unit's report[2] covered school exclusion and non-attendance as twin issues and found similar groups of pupils were at risk of both. School exclusion and non-attendance could also put pupils at risk of social exclusion. This section does not enter into the legal requirements of registration procedures, but rather covers attendance insofar as it is a behaviour issue.

Pupils at risk

Circular 10/99 brings a new perspective on school practice by highlighting vulnerability. Pupils are vulnerable, or at risk of failing in school for a variety of reasons. This may manifest itself through non-attendance, disaffection or academic under-performance. Schools are now required to work together with other agencies, to address or at least take account of these factors when dealing with pupils.

When a pupil is at risk of permanent exclusion, a Pastoral Support Programme (PSP) needs to be set up to document and facilitate this coordinated response. In setting up a PSP the guidelines in the Circular 10/99 must be followed. This perspective on disaffected pupils and the guidance that follows from it forms an important and developing aspect of behaviour policies.

---

[1] OFSTED Handbook for Inspecting Primary and Nursery Schools, p.150. Handbook for Inspecting Secondary Schools, p.138.
[2] Social Exclusion Unit (1998) Truancy and School Exclusion.

SEN – emotional and behavioural difficulties

Pupils with SEN because of emotional and behavioural difficulties (EBD), if they are at risk of exclusion, will also require a PSP, or at least their Individual Educational Plans (IEP) will need to fulfil the same criteria as a PSP. Many of these pupils will be in vulnerable groups, and particularly at risk of disaffection and perhaps exclusion.

There has been an ongoing debate about the causes and definition of pupils presenting behaviour management difficulties in school and by implication the appropriate response.

In some schools, typically in primary practice, children who present serious management difficulties may have been dealt with under SEN procedures, and an Individual Education Plan (IEP) drawn up, often renamed as Individual Behaviour Plan (IBP). In relatively few of the most serious cases, the pupil may have been given a Statement following a statutory assessment, stipulating additional provision, possibly a place at a special school for EBD.

On the other hand, especially in secondary schools, pupils with behaviour difficulties may have been dealt with more frequently through the pastoral or disciplinary system. Persistent and/or severe problems would be managed by imposing fixed term and finally permanent exclusion.

Both of these approaches tend to focus attention on the individual child. In fact, it is generally accepted that within-child factors are only one of the possible causes of behaviour difficulties. Attention also needs to be given to the social and environmental context, including within-school factors, which may be a prime cause or at least an exacerbating factor.

Although Circular 10/99 draws a distinction between disaffected pupils and pupils with emotional and behavioural difficulties, the appropriate response is ultimately the same if a pupil is at risk of exclusion – a PSP (or an IEP that fulfils the same criteria as a PSP). It is up to the school to decide whether the response will be coordinated through the disciplinary or pastoral system or through the SENCO.

It may be that the category of pupils defined as having emotional and behavioural difficulties will be increasingly confined to a relatively small number of pupils with 'diagnosed' disorders such as ADHD, school phobia etc. In pursuing the aim of social inclusion, good practice in terms of the whole school should increasingly provide adequate support for pupils who are vulnerable, including those with special educational needs. This complements the idea that good practice for special educational needs is good practice for all. As the principle of inclusion increasingly informs good practice, fewer pupils will reject, or feel rejected by, schools.

Summary of Guidance

The Summary of Guidance in this Manual (pages 9 to 29) provides an overview of advice pertaining to each aspect. The criteria in the Schedule have been derived directly from this guidance. It covers all the main requirements and recommendations with references to sources, to enable more detailed follow-up for example where the advice extends beyond the remit of behaviour policy. The Summary of Guidance for each aspect is set out separately across a double page spread.

The Schedule

Traditionally, management of change in schools has tended to take the form of analysing both strengths and weaknesses as a basis for future action. However, this frequently leads to focusing on the weaknesses and specifying action to remedy those weaknesses.

The Schedule provides an opportunity to put any difficulties into a wider perspective by identifying and evaluating existing good practice that can be built on. Often, working on behaviour can be threatening and can easily create defensive rather than creative attitudes. Completing the Schedule and acting on its findings is more likely to be a non-threatening process and therefore provide a more effective means to achieve the desired ends.

This solution-focused method is beginning to be used in a variety of ways in educational settings, from helping individual pupils in behaviour and learning, to assisting whole school organisations to embrace change[3].

The Schedule contains the criteria derived directly from the guidance summarised in this Manual for each aspect. Given the reality of the ever-increasing workload on teachers and demands to take on board new initiatives, the Schedule will help identify priorities for action, which are then recorded. On completion, the Schedule provides the school's record of:

- existing strengths on which to build;
- evaluation against recognised criteria;
- priority areas for development.

When the behaviour policy is reviewed again in the future, the Schedule will provide:

- a record of additional strengths that have been developed;
- new priority areas for development;
- evaluation against the same fixed criteria;
- a record of improvement over time.

Each aspect in the Schedule is set out across a double page spread, as in this Manual. This is designed so that the guidance for each aspect can be placed alongside the Schedule for ease of reference whilst it is being completed.

The head teacher could complete the Schedule alone, but it is strongly recommended that as many people as is practical are involved in this review and evaluation. Not everyone may be able to complete every section, but they can be invited to complete the parts where they feel confident.

Completing the Schedule
The Schedule purposely utilises a very similar format to the OFSTED Form S3, i.e. self-evaluations are made against statements to which the responses are 'Fully in place', 'Partly in place' or 'Not in place' (OFSTED has '…with improvement needed' after 'Partly in place'). Complete the Schedule by placing a tick in the relevant box in the grid to indicate where the school is at present in this aspect. At the end of each aspect, an overall judgement is invited, on a scale of 1 to 10, depending on which boxes have been ticked.

Next, consider whether improvement needs to be made in this aspect, and if so, enter a number on the same scale of 1 to 10, to represent where the school aims to be by the next review.

Consider what action needs to be taken to achieve this target and enter identified action/s (or possibilities) into the space provided.

The development plan
Actions identified in the Schedule are prioritised and selectively transferred to the corresponding section in the development plan, where responsibility and timescale are also recorded. This process encourages:

---

[3] Rhodes, J. & Ajmal, Y. (1995) Solution Focused Thinking in Schools, BT Press.

- the development of systems rather than individual troubleshooting – making improvements available to all pupils, not just those demanding attention;
- the recording of action taken;
- the development of explicit links from evaluation to action planning and improvement.

Note that not all the aspects will appear in the development plan. It is more effective to choose two or three aspects to prioritise. The action taken will, in any case, affect several more aspects of the policy anyway. When the time for review comes, it is necessary to complete the whole of the schedule again in order to appreciate the full impact of the action taken.

Completing the development plan

Enter two or three aspects in the first column that have been prioritised for action when completing the Schedule.

Copy into the second column the action/s identified in the Schedule that will bring about the desired improvement.

It may be possible to name the person responsible for the action taking place in the responsibility column.

Put in the suggested date for review.

This summary development plan is not intended to replace the school's existing development planning structure. It is intended to provide a convenient framework to summarise draft proposals within a similar format to the school development plan. Once agreed, they can be easily transferred and included in the normal development planning cycle in the school.

On or before the review date, the whole Schedule needs to be completed again. This will evaluate the outcome of previous action and identify new priorities.

The completed Schedule and proposed development plan can usefully be used as the basis for discussion with whole staff or the governing body, and for deciding together when the next full review needs to take place.

The whole process

1. As many people as practicable complete the Schedule, or the parts that relate to them.
2. A working group collates the results, and on that basis prioritises aspects for development.
3. The working group drafts the development plan for consultation.
4. Responsibilities and time scales are agreed.
5. The development plan is put into action and monitored.
6. At the time specified for review, return to 1.

As the cycle is completed it is most important that successes are celebrated.

Documentation

The Summary of Guidance takes account of the following documentation:

DfEE (2000)
Bullying - don't suffer in silence. An anti-bullying pack for schools.
The previous anti-bullying pack has been updated and circulated to all schools.

DfEE (2000)
SEN Code of Practice on the Identification and Assessment of Pupils with Special Educational Needs (Draft)
The Draft Code of Practice may change as a result of consultation – the final version is to be published in 2001.

Department of Health (DH) & DfEE (2000)
Guidance on the Education of Children and Young People in Public Care
This guidance supercedes Circular 13/94, 'The Education of Children being looked after by Local Authorities', which was in the 'Pupils with Problems' pack. It advises on the role of local authorities, including schools, as corporate parents, particularly in regard to education.

OFSTED (1999)
Inspecting Schools, The Framework
OFSTED (1999)
Handbook for Inspecting Primary and Nursery Schools & Handbook for Inspecting Secondary Schools
The OFSTED Framework sets out the requirements for the inspection of schools and the handbooks provide guidance for inspectors on the application of the framework, including the criteria by which judgements will be made.

DfEE (1999)
Circular 10/99 Social Inclusion: Pupil Support
Governors have a legal obligation to have regard to this circular. It is the most recent DfEE guidance to schools on behaviour policy and exclusions, replacing Circular 8/94 and 10/94 from the 'Pupils with Problems' pack. It concentrates mainly on appropriate action when there are behaviour difficulties, including non-attendance and notably introduced the provision of Pastoral Support Programmes (PSPs).

Daniels, H., Visser, J., Cole, T. & de Reybekill, N.
Emotional and Behavioural Difficulties in Mainstream Schools (1999)
Research Report No. 90, DfEE
A study commissioned to identify effective practice in the assessment and provision for children with emotional and behavioural difficulties in mainstream schools. A summary is contained in a 'Research Brief'.

DfEE (1998)
Home School Agreements: Guidance for Schools
Statutory guidance on all aspects of home-school agreements.

Social Exclusion Unit (1998)
Truancy and School Exclusion
An influential report from the Government-appointed unit, outlining underlying factors and good practice in reducing truancy and school exclusion.

School Standards and Framework Act 1998
HMSO
Carrying some provisions on behaviour forward from the 1997 Education Act, it includes further legislation on behaviour policies, attendance targets, exclusions, home-school agreements and work experience for Key Stage 4 pupils.

Human Rights Act 1998
HMSO
The Human Rights Act came into force in 2000.

Education Act 1997
HMSO
This Act includes the law on detention and LEA behaviour support plans.

DfE (1994)
Pupils with Problems, Circulars 9/94 The Education of Children with EBD
This circular is still current but with a review pending.

Aspects of behaviour policy –
Summary of Guidance

Throughout these sections, actual quotations from documents are in italics.
Sources are given in the left-hand column.

Aspect 1

Aims and principles for the behaviour policy

> **The governing body should make a written statement of general principles which sets the framework for the school's behaviour policy.**

Schools have twin aims in educating their pupils – to promote learning and achievement and to prepare pupils for life. Good behaviour policy and practice will reflect these aims. Effective teaching and learning can only take place in an atmosphere that is purposeful and calm. The values that we promote in school should prepare pupils for the responsibilities and opportunities of life.

School Standards and Framework Act 1998 Part II Chapter V section 61

The 1998 Act places the responsibility on the governing body to ensure that policies are pursued to promote good behaviour. The governing body must make, and from time to time review, *a written statement of general principles to which the head teacher is to have regard in determining any measures* to promote good behaviour in school.

According to the legislation the values or principles that the behaviour policy should promote include:
* *self-discipline and proper regard for authority;*
* *respect for others ... and in particular, preventing all forms of bullying among pupils.*

OFSTED Framework p.42

OFSTED states that one criterion for judging how well the school is led and managed is that:
The school has explicit aims and values, including a commitment to good relationships and equality of opportunity for all, which are reflected in all its work.

OFSTED Framework p.39

OFSTED Handbook: Primary p.72 Secondary p.68

OFSTED inspectors will assess to what extent the school:
* *promotes principles which distinguish between right and wrong;*
* *promotes such values as honesty, fairness and respect for truth and justice.*

Governing bodies must have regard to the statutory guidance in Circular 10/99 Social Inclusion: Pupil Support.

DfEE Circular 10/99 Social Inclusion: Pupil Support Annex B para 2

Circular 10/99 advises the governors' statement should cover:
* *the ethos of the school, its values and the boundaries of acceptable behaviour;*
* *the school's moral code;*
* *positive and constructive rules of conduct;*
* *the rewards and punishments to be fairly and consistently applied.*

School Standards and
Framework Act 1998 Part II
Chapter V section 61

Before they make or revise the statement of principles the governing body must *consult the head teacher and parents of registered pupils.*

DfEE Circular 10/99 Social
Inclusion: Pupil Support
Annex B para 3

Circular 10/99 Annex B suggests that *consultation could be at their (the governors') annual general meeting for parents or at a specially convened meeting, or in writing.*

Schools have fulfilled the requirements to consult in different ways. Some have included aims and principles as an introduction in the behaviour policy and consulted on the whole policy with parents. Others have included the principles in the home-school agreement consultation, thereby covering both the general principles and the home-school agreement together.

DfEE Circular 10/99 Social
Inclusion: Pupil Support
Annex B para 2

Circular 10/99 recommends that the statement of general principles should take account of *the needs of all pupils, including any with special educational needs.*

DfEE Circular 10/99 Social
Inclusion: Pupil Support
Annex B para 5

The governing body should also advise the head teacher of their views on particular matters, such as *bullying, racial or sexual harassment, and maintaining regular attendance.*

School Standards and
Framework Act 1998 Part II
Chapter V section 61

According to the Act, *the making of rules and provision for enforcing them* is the head teacher's rather than governors' responsibility – however, the governing body may recommend that rules, rewards and sanctions are among measures the head teacher should take.

DfEE Circular 10/99 Social
Inclusion: Pupil Support
Annex B para 4

The governing body should oversee the head teacher's sound maintenance of discipline at the school in line with their policies.

Aspect 2

Promoting the ethos of good behaviour

> **The head teacher documents in the behaviour policy what measures are taken to promote high standards of behaviour and ensures everyone knows what they are.**

The head teacher has a legal duty to decide on the measures to be taken in school to promote good behaviour, and eliminate all forms of bullying, taking into account the governors' advice and statement of principles.

School Standards and Framework Act 1998 Part II Chapter V section 61

The measures determined by the head teacher … shall be publicised by him in the form of a written document.

He shall make the measures generally known within the school and to parents … and, at least once in every school year … bring them to the attention of all … pupils, parents and all employed, or otherwise engaged to provide their services, at the school.

In other words, it is the head teacher's legal responsibility to ensure the school has a written behaviour policy that is widely known and regularly drawn to attention.

DfEE Circular 10/99 Social Inclusion: Pupil Support Annex B para 7

DfEE Circular 10/99 advises that this written policy needs to be available in other relevant languages if English is not the first language of many of the parents, in order to meet the requirement to publicise the policy to all parents.

DfEE Circular 10/99 Social Inclusion: Pupil Support Annex B para 8

The discipline policy should:
- *define the standards of behaviour the school wants to achieve;*
- *seek the widest possible measure of agreement on these standards and how to achieve them;*
- *ensure that these standards are consistently and fairly applied throughout the school.*

DfEE Circular 10/99 Social Inclusion: Pupil Support 2.1

It is good practice to involve pupils in reinforcing the behaviour policy by contributing ideas through schools' councils and in class discussions.

OFSTED Handbook Primary p.42 Secondary p.40

OFSTED Inspectors may ask
… if pupils contributed to the behaviour policy or know about it.

DfEE Circular 10/99 Social Inclusion: Pupil Support Chapter 2.1

DfEE Circular 10/99 outlines key good practice principles as:
- *Setting good habits early* (primary schools, regular and punctual attendance, involving parents);
- *Early intervention* (for unexplained absence and behaviour);

- *Rewarding achievements* (positive recognition, especially in primary schools);
- *Supporting behaviour management* (techniques such as Circle Time, Circle of Friends, Assertive Discipline);
- *Working with parents* (home-school agreements, parents' meetings, newsletters);
- *Involving pupils* (anti-bullying and harassment, school's councils, discussions);
- *Commitment to equal opportunities* (equal opportunities policy and monitoring);
- *Identifying underlying causes* (additional literacy or numeracy support);
- *Study support* (homework clubs, thinking skills workshops, family support services).

OFSTED inspections judge to what extent curricular and other opportunities that are provided by school help pupils' personal and social development.

OFSTED Framework p.39

Inspectors should consider the extent to which the school provides curricular and other opportunities that:
- *encourage pupils to take responsibility, show initiative and develop an understanding of living in a community;*
- *provide effectively for personal and social education, including health education, sex education and attention to drug misuse.*

OFSTED Handbook:
Secondary p.60
Primary p.66

The curriculum cannot be satisfactory if ... it does little to inculcate respect, tolerance and good behaviour.

The legislation, guidance and good practice intend to ensure that the whole school community, including parents, are aware of the aims and principles themselves, decided by the governing body. Moreover they need to be aware of the measures taken to fulfil those aims, decided by the head teacher. It is the head teacher's responsibility to make sure of this awareness and secure the widest agreement. Both would be included, for example, in the home-school agreement. The head teacher ensures the general principles are promoted throughout the life of the school.

OFSTED Handbook:
Primary p.72
Secondary p.68

The school should provide *a moral code as a basis for behaviour which is promoted throughout the life of the school.*

Aspect 3

The code of conduct – rules, rewards and sanctions

> **The behaviour policy should make clear the rules, rewards and sanctions that will promote the standards of behaviour the school wants to achieve.**

DfEE Circular 10/99 Social Inclusion: Pupil Support Annex B para 1

The behaviour policy should make clear:
- *the boundaries of what is acceptable;*
- *the hierarchy of sanctions;*
- *a linked system of rewards for good behaviour.*

DfEE Circular 10/99 Social Inclusion: Pupil Support Annex B para 8

When drawing up the policy the head teacher should:
- *seek the widest possible measure of agreement on these standards and how to achieve them;*
- *ensure that these standards are consistently and fairly applied throughout the school.*

In other words the head teacher needs to put in place monitoring procedures to ensure consistency and fairness.

DfEE Circular 10/99 Social Inclusion: Pupil Support Annex B para 2

The school rules should be *positive and constructive.*

Circular 10/99 concentrates more on good practice when dealing with difficult behaviour than on preventive measures. However, the *key principles* of good practice are more proactive and include:

DfEE Circular 10/99 Social Inclusion: Pupil Support 2.1

Rewarding achievements: positive recognition of individual pupil, class or year group achievements in good attendance and behaviour, through mentions in assembly, awarding certificates or prizes, is helpful especially in primary schools.

DfEE Circular 10/99 Social Inclusion: Pupil Support 4.11

DfEE Circular 10/99 Social Inclusion: Pupil Support Annex B para 8

Sanctions should be applied:
- *fairly and consistently;*
- *taking account of all circumstances including the child's age;*
- *within a context of positive reinforcement of good behaviour;*
- *in proportion to offences and enable pupils to make reparation where appropriate.*

DfEE Circular 10/99 Social Inclusion: Pupil Support 4.11

A list of possible sanctions is given in Circular 10/99:
- *removal from the group (in class);*
- *withdrawal of break or lunchtime privileges;*
- *detention;*
- *withholding participation in any school trips or sports events that are not an essential part of the curriculum;*
- *withdrawal from, for example, a particular lesson or peer group;*
- *completion of assigned work or extra written work;*
- *carrying out a useful task in the school.*

DfEE Circular 10/99 Social
Inclusion: Pupil Support
4.12

Punishments that are humiliating or degrading should not be used.

Human Rights Act, 1998
Article 3

Inhuman or degrading treatment or punishment would contravene the Human Rights Act.

DfEE Circular 10/99 Social
Inclusion: Pupil Support
Annex D para 2

Lunchtime bans, if used as a sanction, should have been previously determined and been made known, as any other of the head teacher's measures. A free school meal, which could be a packed lunch, must be provided if the pupil is entitled. Normally a lunchtime ban would be for no more than five days.

Education Act 1997
Chapter 44 Part II
section 5

also

DfEE Circular 10/99 Social
Inclusion: Pupil Support
Annex C

The position on detention was clarified in the 1997 Education Act, which allows the use of detention, although under certain constraints. Detention of a pupil after the end of any school session without parental consent is not illegal if:
- parents are given at least 24 hours notice in writing;
- detention has been previously determined as one of the head teacher's measures, and has been made generally known;
- it is given by the head or a teacher authorised by the head.

It must also be reasonable, in terms of the punishment being proportionate and in terms of any special circumstances, in particular:
- the pupil's age;
- any special educational needs;
- any religious requirements;
- whether suitable travel arrangements, if necessary, can reasonably be made by parents.

(For use of exclusion see Aspect 8 Pupils at risk)

Aspect 4

Partnership with parents/carers

> The school should build a partnership with parents so they support the school in promoting good behaviour and attendance.

School Standards and Framework Act 1998 Part II Chapter V section 61

The promotion of partnership with parents (or carers) has been strengthened by recent legislation. The governing body must consult parents before making or revising the statement of general principles for the behaviour policy and the policy must be made known to parents – and be brought to their attention at least once in every school year.

School Standards and Framework Act 1998 Part IV section 110

The home-school agreement, with a parental declaration, is subject to parental consultation.

School Standards and Framework Act 1998 Part IV section 110

All governing bodies should have adopted a home-school agreement, which needs to be reviewed from time to time, specifying:
- the school's aims and values;
- the school's responsibilities;
- the parental responsibilities;
- the school's expectations of the pupils' conduct.

The school's aims and values are at least partly set out in the governors' statement of general principles for the behaviour policy.

School Standards and Framework Act 1998 Part IV section 111

Although the agreement sets out the parents' responsibilities, a pupil cannot be excluded or suffer any adverse consequences as a result of parents' failure to sign a parental declaration and signing the parental declaration must not be used as a condition of entry to a school.

The governing body is under a legal duty to have regard to guidance from the Secretary of State in the DfEE publication *Home-School Agreements: Guidance for Schools.*

DfEE Home-School Agreements: Guidance for Schools para 6

The most successful and workable agreements arise out of and are clearly linked to the school's policies and practices. They are part of a whole school approach to partnership with parents and pupils.

DfEE Circular 10/99 Social Inclusion: Pupil Support 2.1

One of the key principles of good practice is:
Working with Parents: all schools should encourage parents to support good attendance and behaviour through home-school agreements, parents' meetings and newsletters.

DfEE Circular 10/99 Social
Inclusion: Pupil Support
3.16-17

Times of transition, from home to infant school or at the transfer from primary to middle or secondary school can be unsettling for children. Communication and contact with parents is central in easing pupils through changes.

DfEE Circular 10/99 Social
Inclusion: Pupil Support
3.13-14

Children are at particular risk of disaffection and exclusion if their family is under stress and it should be taken into consideration when dealing with the pupil. Adverse circumstances would include unemployment, bereavement, the loss of one or more parents through divorce or separation, and new adult partnerships.

Other agencies such as Social Services or counselling services may contribute by helping with the underlying family problem, especially where the child may be at risk.

DfEE Circular 10/99 Social
Inclusion: Pupil Support
4.10

Generally staff should involve parents early in problems so they can agree action together.

DfEE Circular 10/99 Social
Inclusion: Pupil Support
2.1

Schools should always know who has parental responsibility for all their pupils.

Guidance on the Education
of Children and Young
People in Public Care

Schools have an important role in 'corporate parenting' and must have a designated person to facilitate additional provision for pupils who are in public care, or 'looked after' by the local authority.

The designated person has the responsibility for maintaining communication with social services, the primary carer and/or with parents where possible. The designated person should act as an advocate in the school for children in public care and should facilitate the Personal Education Plan (PEP) that each of these pupils should have.

Aspect 5

Roles and responsibilities

> The governing body actively promotes the aims and principles that underpin the ethos of the school. The head teacher determines day-to-day policy and practice. Teachers work in ways that minimise disaffection. All staff provide good role models for pupils.

School Standards and Framework Act 1998 Part II Chapter V sections 61, 64-68, 110

The governing body's legal responsibilities include:
* ensuring policies to promote good behaviour are pursued;
* writing a statement of general principles for the behaviour policy;
* advising the head teacher on particular measures;
* establishing a discipline committee to consider certain exclusions;
* adopting a home-school agreement and parental declaration.

DfEE Circular 10/99 Social Inclusion: Pupil Support 2.1, 4.5, 4.32 Annex B para 9

The governing body, with the head teacher, should:
* *consider a whole school approach to non-attendance, with particular reference to unauthorised absence;*
* review policies, particularly in regard to anti-bullying, racial and sexual harassment and equal opportunities;
* inform the LEA annually of the pattern and frequency of any racial incidents.

School Standards and Framework Act 1998 Part II Chapter V section 61

The head teacher's legal responsibilities include determining:
* the standard of behaviour regarded as acceptable;
* *measures (which may include making rules and the provision for enforcing them) to promote good behaviour and to prevent all forms of bullying.*

School Standards and Framework Act 1998 Part II Chapter V section 61

The head teacher must:
* *publicise these measures ... in the form of a written document;*
* *make them generally known within the school and to parents;*
* *at least once a year, bring them to the attention of pupils, parents and all employed, or otherwise engaged to provide services, at the school.*

DfEE Circular 10/99 Social Inclusion: Pupil Support Annex B para 4

The head teacher has day to day responsibility (for good behaviour), *with the backing of the governing body.*

DfEE Circular 10/99 Social Inclusion: Pupil Support 4.9

The school's behaviour policy should set out what arrangements are in place to support teachers and other staff when they are dealing with pupils who cause difficulties. These arrangements need to be well understood and effective.

The OFSTED guidance emphasises the importance of group management skills and developing relationships with pupils within the context of a working atmosphere.

OFSTED Handbook:
Secondary p.54
Primary p.59

Teachers can reduce the incidence of inappropriate behaviour by:
- exercising authority clearly and fairly from the outset;
- holding the pupils' attention, involving them in the work and encouraging concentration and completion of the task;
- organising the work and grouping of pupils clearly and efficiently;
- supporting and controlling the pupils, intervening according to need;
- establishing mutual respect and proper habits of work;
- conveying the importance of self-discipline and expectations of mature behaviour.

DfEE Circular 10/99 Social
Inclusion: Pupil Support
4.10-11

When dealing with difficult behaviour teachers should:
- involve and agree action with parents early;
- apply sanctions fairly and consistently within a context of positive reinforcement of good behaviour;
- actively identify pupils who do not respond to school action to combat disaffection and who need a Pastoral Support Plan. (See Aspect 8 Pupils at risk)

DfEE Circular 10/99 Social
Inclusion: Pupil Support
5

DfEE Circular 10/99 Social
Inclusion: Pupil Support
4.30

All teaching staff and non-teaching staff, including lunchtime supervisors, should be alert to signs of bullying and act promptly and firmly.

OFSTED Handbook:
Secondary p.68
Primary p.72

Adults provide powerful role models for children and should, therefore, model the values such as courtesy and respect in all their dealings with other adults and pupils in the school.

Aspect 6

Anti-bullying and harassment

> **Measures should be in place to monitor and prevent all forms of bullying including racial and sexual harassment.**

Human Rights Act, 1998
Article 3

Bullying continues to be a sensitive and important issue for schools. Headteachers need to ensure that school policies uphold human rights: *No one shall be subjected to torture or to inhuman or degrading treatment or punishment.* The term bullying is used in legislation for the first time in the 1998 Act, whereby there is a statutory requirement on head teachers to:

School Standards and
Framework Act 1998 Part II
Chapter V section 61

determine measures to be taken with a view to ... encouraging respect for others and, in particular, preventing all forms of bullying among pupils.

DfEE Circular 10/99 Social
Inclusion: Pupil Support
Annex B 9-10

In Circular 10/99 the DfEE gives guidance on measures that would help fulfil this duty:
* *governing bodies should regularly review their school anti-bullying policy;*
* *prospectuses and other documents for staff, pupils and parents should explain arrangements for pupils to report bullying to staff and how staff will investigate them.*

DfEE Circular 10/99 Social
Inclusion: Pupil Support
2.1

Other recommended anti-bullying measures found in Circular 10/99 include the involvement of pupils by:
* active involvement in anti-bullying and harassment policies;
* contributing ideas through schools' councils and in class discussions;

DfEE Circular 10/99 Social
Inclusion: Pupil Support
4.20 & 4.29

* supporting younger pupils being bullied;
* reporting bullying to staff or to older pupils they can trust.

DfEE Circular 10/99 Social
Inclusion: Pupil Support
4.30

The anti-bullying policy should ensure that:
* all teaching and non-teaching staff, including lunchtime supervisors, are alert to signs of bullying;
* all staff act promptly and firmly when alerted to an incidence of bullying;
* strategies cover play and break time;
* all relevant staff receive appropriate training;
* staff are aware of vulnerable pupils e.g. pupils in public care, refugee children, children for whom English is a second language.

Home-School Agreements:
Guidance for Schools
para 20

Home-school agreements *should make clear that the pupil will be expected to observe the school's discipline and anti-bullying policy.*

Measures to combat racial harassment have more prominence than previously in both DfEE and OFSTED guidance.

DfEE Circular 10/99 Social
Inclusion: Pupil Support
2.1

A key principle is the explicit commitment to equal opportunities. *Schools should monitor the impact of their policies and procedures on different groups (by race, gender and disability) and effectiveness assessed at governors' meetings.*

DfEE Circular 10/99 Social
Inclusion: Pupil Support
4.32

All schools' behaviour policies must make clear that racial harassment will not be tolerated and say how staff and pupils should deal with it. The school should record all racial incidents, and parents and governors should be informed of such incidents and the action taken to deal with them. Governing bodies should inform LEAs annually of the pattern and frequency of any incidents. Pupils who have suffered racial harassment, at or outside school, may need support.

DfEE Circular 10/99 Social
Inclusion: Pupil Support
4.33

Sexual harassment is most often carried out by boys against girls. Personal, Social & Health Education can help to foster appropriate and responsible sexual behaviour and deter offensive behaviour.

OFSTED Handbook:
Secondary p.76
Primary p.80

The emphasis in the OFSTED Handbooks is often on the proactive teaching of personal development directly through personal and social education, through the delivery of the curriculum and through the role models that staff and other adults provide. As part of the inspection of how well the school cares for its pupils an inspection should *assess the impact of the school's statutory behaviour policy in promoting respect and tolerance towards others and their beliefs, cultures and ethnic backgrounds.*

OFSTED Handbook:
Secondary p.76
Primary p.80

Inspectors should also check the policy to ensure the requirements of Circular 10/99 (above) are in place and may *ask for the records of any incidents that have taken place during the previous 12 months.*

OFSTED Handbook:
Secondary p.38
Primary p.40

Attitudes, values and personal development … cannot be satisfactory if there are more than isolated instances of:
- *disruptive, aggressive or intimidating behaviour; or*
- *racist attitudes or sexist language or behaviour.*

DfEE Don't suffer in silence –
An anti-bullying pack for schools
p.22 and p.24

The issue of bullying in schools was fully explored in the DfE Sheffield project. This culminated in an anti-bullying pack for schools, recently updated, giving guidance on preventive approaches and particular strategies for responding to incidents. This pack advises that:
- *Where other strategies do not resolve the problem, permanent exclusion may be justified in the most serious and persistent cases, particularly where violence is involved.*
- *Where serious violence is involved, the headteacher can and should normally permanently exclude a pupil.*

Aspect 7

Attendance

> Schools need to take a whole school approach to promote good attendance and to monitor any unauthorised absence so that prompt action can be taken.

DfEE Circular 10/99 Social Inclusion: Pupil Support 2.1

In Circular 10/99 attendance is mentioned several times in the key principles to good practice:
- *Setting good habits early* (primary schools need to establish regular punctual attendance involving parents);
- *Early intervention* (prompt intervention for unexplained absence);
- *Rewarding achievements* (achievements in good attendance through mentions in assembly, awarding certificates or prizes especially in primary school);
- *Working with parents* (encouraging parents to support good attendance and behaviour through home-school agreements, parents' meetings and newsletters).

DfEE Circular 10/99 Social Inclusion: Pupil Support 4.5

Governing bodies and head teachers have a particular role in considering a whole school approach to non-attendance, with particular reference to unauthorised absence.

DfEE Circular 10/99 Social Inclusion: Pupil Support 4.4

Schools should closely monitor unauthorised absence so that any patterns, including missing individual lessons, are acted on.

DfEE Circular 10/99 Social Inclusion: Pupil Support 4.2

School administrative staff or volunteers should contact parents on any day a registered pupil of compulsory school age is absent without explanation, including in cases where the pupil skips lessons after registration.

In addition it is vital that any unauthorised absence is addressed early on through discussion between a pupil and the teacher responsible for the pupil's registration.

DfEE Circular 10/99 Social Inclusion: Pupil Support 4.3

Other approaches recommended are:
- using IT to monitor attendance;
- raising the profile of attendance with parents;
- regularly reminding parents of procedures for notifying absence and school policy on holidays in term time;
- attendance checks, particularly for post-registration truancy;
- having a senior member of staff responsible for attendance;
- pupil passes confirming authority to be out of school;
- group work with irregular attenders and with their parents.

DfEE Circular 10/99 Social Inclusion: Pupil Support 4.6

There should be clear criteria in place for referring pupils to the LEA Education Welfare Service.

DfEE Circular 10/99 Social
Inclusion: Pupil Support
4.7-8

Schools should work together with other community groups on initiatives such as truancy watch schemes that can be supported by:
- *the new police power to take truants found in public areas back to school or wherever specified by the LEA;*
- *leaflet campaigns for parents;*
- *publicity in local shopping centres or on buses;*
- *pupil pass schemes;*
- *truancy hotlines;*
- *'truancy-free zone' posters in shops and information packs for retail staff.*

OFSTED Handbook:
Primary p.45
Secondary p.43

Attendance is included in the OFSTED evaluation of *'Pupils' attitudes, values and personal development'*. In primary schools inspectors only need make further inquiries if the attendance is below 95%, or showing a downward trend. At secondary level the threshold is 92% or below 90% in any year group.

Inspectors may inquire about how parents support regular attendance and whether the school:
- *has straightforward procedures for reporting absence;*
- *conforms to guidance on completion of registers;*
- *works with the Education Welfare Service;*
- *analyses attendance data, especially if there are differences between year or ethnic groups;*
- *compares its data on attendance with other similar schools.*

OFSTED Handbook:
Primary p.80

In the primary phase the priority which the staff gives to encouraging good attendance and behaviour is a strong indicator of the steps taken by the school to ensure pupils' welfare and safety.

DfEE Circular 10/99 Social
Inclusion: Pupil Support 4.1

Children who do not attend school without authorisation are putting themselves at risk.

Aspect 8

Pupils at risk

> Children at risk of failing in school should be actively identified and strategies adopted, in collaboration with parents and other agencies where appropriate.

DfEE Circular 10/99 Social Inclusion: Pupil Support 3.1-19, 4.1

Certain pupils are at particular risk, for example:
- those with special educational needs;
- children in the care of local authorities;
- minority ethnic children;
- Travellers;
- young carers;
- those from families under stress;
- pregnant schoolgirls and teenage mothers;
- all pupils in transition from one stage of education to another;
- pupils entering school outside the normal year of entry;
- refugee children;
- those who do not attend without authorisation.

DfEE Circular 10/99 Social Inclusion: Pupil Support p.17

Schools should regularly review the progress of pupils. In particular they should carry out a check no later than the end of Year 9 to identify any pupils at risk of failure in school, in partnership with the Careers Service, Education Welfare Officers and other agencies.

DfEE Circular 10/99 Social Inclusion: Pupil Support 4.9-36

Strategies for dealing with disruptive behaviour include:
- arrangements for supporting staff;
- working with parents;
- sanctions;
- in-school centres;
- mentoring;
- curricular flexibility, including disapplication of national curriculum, work-related learning, college placements, voluntary or community activities.

DfEE Circular 10/99 Social Inclusion: Pupil Support 4.28-30

Special strategies may be required, including collaborating with other agencies, where the behaviour involves:
- drugs;
- bullying or racial and sexual harassment;
- crime.

DfEE Circular 10/99 Social Inclusion: Pupil Support Chapter 5

A Pastoral Support Programme (PSP) should be set up for pupils who do not respond to these strategies and are at serious risk of permanent exclusion or criminal activity or otherwise failing at school through disaffection. A PSP should:
- *be overseen by a nominated member of staff;*
- *be short and practical and administration kept to a minimum;*

24

DfEE Circular 10/99 Social Inclusion: Pupil Support 5.6	The school should consider: • *putting in place a programme for learning difficulties;* • *disapplying the National Curriculum;* • *changing the child's teaching set or class;* • *jointly registering the pupil at a Pupil Referral Unit;* • *a managed move to another school;* • *outside expertise e.g. for bereavement or drug dependency;* • *placing the child in a support unit.*

• *be discussed and agreed with parents;*
• *be discussed and agreed with an LEA representative;*
• *involve other agencies as appropriate.*

DfEE Circular 10/99 Social Inclusion: Pupil Support 5.6

The school should consider:
• *putting in place a programme for learning difficulties;*
• *disapplying the National Curriculum;*
• *changing the child's teaching set or class;*
• *jointly registering the pupil at a Pupil Referral Unit;*
• *a managed move to another school;*
• *outside expertise e.g. for bereavement or drug dependency;*
• *placing the child in a support unit.*

DfEE Circular 10/99 Social Inclusion: Pupil Support 5.7

The PSP should include:
• *precise and realistic behavioural outcomes broken down into fortnightly tasks;*
• *the rewards for meeting the targets and the sanctions if certain behaviour occurs;*
• *if it has a time limit, a review at least halfway through.*

DfEE Circular 10/99 Social Inclusion: Pupil Support 5.5 & 2.2-5

Schools should work in collaboration with a wide range of other agencies such as social services, housing departments, youth services, voluntary organisations, careers services, ethnic minority community groups, education welfare service, educational psychologists, health workers, mental health services, behaviour support teams and Youth Offending Teams.

DfEE Circular 10/99 Social Inclusion: Pupil Support 6.2

A pupil should only be excluded – fixed period or permanently:
• *in response to serious breaches of the discipline policy;*
• *once a range of alternative strategies have been tried and have failed;*
• *if allowing the pupil to remain in school would seriously harm the education or welfare of the pupil or other pupils.*

DfEE Circular 10/99 Social Inclusion: Pupil Support 6.6

A PSP should have been used before a decision is taken to exclude a pupil permanently.

DfEE Don't suffer in silence – An anti-bullying pack for schools, p.22

The recent anti-bullying pack for schools advises that: *where other strategies do not resolve the problem, permanent exclusion may be justified in the most serious and persistent cases, particularly where violence is involved.*

Aspect 9

SEN – emotional and behavioural difficulties

> **Pupils with emotional and behavioural difficulties need approaches that are an extension of the whole school behaviour policy, working in partnership with parents, pupils and other agencies.**

Circular 9/94 para 2	The generally accepted definition of emotional and behavioural difficulties that constitute special educational needs can be found in DfEE Circular 9/94: *emotional and behavioural difficulties lie on the continuum between behaviour which challenges teachers but is within normal, albeit unacceptable, bounds and that which is indicative of serious mental illness.*
Circular 9/94 para 3	*Whether or not a child is judged to have emotional and behavioural difficulties will depend on the nature, frequency, persistence, severity or abnormality and cumulative effect of the behaviour, in context, compared to normal expectations for a child of the age concerned.*
Circular 9/94 para 3	There needs to be clear procedures so that staff actively identify pupils whose behaviour is causing concern. Pupils' initial behavioural needs should normally be met within *the context of the school's behaviour management policy.*
DfEE Draft SEN Code of Practice 5.5, 6.5	Schools should adopt a graduated response that includes a wide array of strategies.
DfEE Draft SEN Code of Practice 5.12, 6.12	The teacher, after consultation with the parents, should consider with the SENCO whether *School Action* is required. The trigger for intervention through *School Action* is when the child *despite receiving differentiated learning opportunities ... presents persistent emotional or behavioural difficulties which are not ameliorated by the behaviour management techniques usually employed in the school.* All relevant information about the child should be collected, including contacting outside agencies such as Social Services or Health that are working with the child.
DfEE Draft SEN Code of Practice 5.12, 6.12	The SENCO (or link SENCO in secondary schools) should take the lead in assessment, planning, monitoring and reviewing.
DfEE Draft SEN Code of Practice 5.12, 6.12	Parents must always be consulted and kept informed of the action taken and of the outcome.

DfEE Draft SEN Code of Practice 5.14, 6.14	Strategies employed should be recorded within an Individual Education Plan (IEP). The IEP should include: • *the short-term targets set for the child/pupil;* • *the teaching strategies to be used;* • *the provision to be put in place;* • *when the plan is to be reviewed;* • *the outcome of the action taken.* *The IEP should be discussed with the child/pupil and the parents.*
DfEE Draft SEN Code of Practice 5.16, 6.16	The trigger for *School Action Plus* is if despite these strategies under *School Action* the pupil *has emotional or behavioural difficulties which substantially and regularly interfere with the child's own learning or that of the class group, despite having an individualised behaviour management programme.*
DfEE Draft SEN Code of Practice 5.16, 6.16	At *School Action Plus* external support services advise on more specialist strategies, assessments and targets. The delivery of the new IEP continues to be the responsibility of the class/subject teachers and *should usually be implemented, at least in part and as far as possible, in the normal classroom setting.*
DfEE Circular 10/99 Social Inclusion: Pupil Support 5.3	Pupils with SEN who are at risk of exclusion should have a Pastoral Support Programme or an IEP that fulfils the same criteria laid down in Circular 10/99 for a PSP (see Aspect 8).
DfEE Circular 10/99 Social Inclusion: Pupil Support 6.10, 6.12	Head teachers should avoid permanently excluding pupils with Statements, or part-way through the assessment process, other than in the most exceptional circumstances. *Schools should try every practicable means to maintain placements, including seeking LEA and other professional advice as appropriate. Where this process has been exhausted, the school should liaise with the LEA about initiating an 'interim' annual review of the Statement.*
DfEE Research Report 90 (Research Brief)	Although children with behaviour difficulties provide the most challenging aspect of inclusion, it is important to remember that *effective teaching skills for pupils with EBD are the same as those for all pupils.*

Aspect 10

The pupils' response

> The pupils respond to the school's policies and practice by demonstrating
> a high standard of behaviour that maximises their learning.

This section is drawn entirely from the OFSTED Framework and guidance for schools. The 'acid test' of behaviour policies and practice is how the pupils actually behave.

Under the heading of *Pupils' Attitudes, Values and Personal Development*, the Framework describes four areas to be evaluated and the criteria by which these are judged.

OFSTED Framework p.37

Attitudes to the school will be judged by considering the extent to which pupils:
- *are keen and eager to come to school;*
- *show interest in school life and are involved in the range of activities the school provides.*

Behaviour, including the incidence of exclusions, will be judged by considering the extent to which pupils:
- *behave well in lessons and around the school;*
- *are courteous;*
- *are trustworthy;*
- *show respect for property.*

Personal development and relationships will be judged by considering the extent to which pupils:
- *form constructive relationships with one another;*
- *form constructive relationships with teachers and other adults;*
- *work in an atmosphere free from oppressive behaviour such as bullying, sexism and racism;*
- *reflect on what they do and understand the impact of their actions on others;*
- *respect other people's differences, particularly their feelings, values and beliefs;*
- *show initiative;*
- *are willing to take responsibility.*

Attendance will be judged by considering the extent to which pupils *have high levels of attendance.*

OFSTED Framework p.38

When determining their judgements on *How well are pupils or students taught?* inspectors will judge the quality of teaching and how well pupils learn and make progress. Inspectors will consider the extent to which pupils:

28

- *apply intellectual, physical or creative effort in their work;*
- *are productive and work at a good pace;*
- *show interest in their work, are able to sustain concentration and think and learn for themselves;*
- *understand what they are doing, how well they have done and how they can improve.*

OFSTED Handbook:
Secondary p.38
Primary p.40

Attitudes, values and personal development ... cannot be satisfactory if there are more than isolated instances of:
- *disruptive, aggressive or intimidating behaviour;*
- *racist attitudes or sexist language or behaviour;*
- *marked unruliness in one or more classes;*

and in secondary schools:
- *significant truancy or lack of punctuality.*

29

BEHAVIOUR POLICY AND PRACTICE: SELF-EVALUATION PACK FOR SCHOOLS

SCHEDULE

Before beginning to use the SCHEDULE and development plan please consult the accompanying MANUAL which gives notes for completing and a Summary of Guidance on each aspect of the behaviour policy evaluation.

Behaviour Policy and Practice:
Self-Evaluation Pack for Schools

SCHEDULE

Contents

Aspects of behaviour policy – evaluation

Aspect 1

Aims and principles for the behaviour policy

> **The governing body should make a written statement of general principles which sets the framework for the school's behaviour policy.**

	Fully in place	Partly in place	Not in place
The governing body has made a written statement of general principles in consultation with the head teacher.			
When making or revising the statement, the governing body consulted with parents.			

The statement of principles promotes values such as:			
self-discipline;			
proper regard for authority;			
respect for others;			
intolerance of bullying and harassment;			
the difference between right and wrong;			
honesty;			
fairness;			
respect for truth and justice;			
equality of opportunity for all.			

The statement of general principles (or a summary) can be found:			
in the behaviour policy;			
in the home-school agreement.			

	Fully in place	Partly in place	Not in place

The statement includes:

the ethos and values of the school;			
the boundaries of acceptable behaviour;			
the school's moral code;			
the provision for rewards and sanctions to be fairly and consistently applied.			

The statement takes account of all pupils, including those with special needs.			

The governing body has advised the head teacher of its views on bullying, racism or sexual harassment, and maintaining attendance.			

The governing body oversees the sound maintenance of discipline.			

Overall evaluation:
On the scale of 0 – 10, where 0 = nothing yet in place, and 10 = everything in place, mark on the scale where you assess the school is at present with this aspect:

```
0     1     2     3     4     5     6     7     8     9     10
```

Is this aspect a priority for development?

If so, where on the scale would you like to be at the next review?

What action will achieve that?

(If prioritised, enter this aspect and identified action into the Development Plan.)

Aspect 2

Promoting the ethos of good behaviour

> The head teacher documents in the behaviour policy what measures are taken to promote high standards of behaviour and ensures everyone knows what they are.

	Fully in place	Partly in place	Not in place

The head teacher has determined measures to promote good behaviour that:	Fully in place	Partly in place	Not in place
form part of the written behaviour policy;			
are generally known within the school and by parents;			
at least once a year, are brought to the attention of pupils, parents and all employed, or otherwise engaged to provide services, at the school.			

The policy is available in relevant languages other than English, where appropriate.			

The policy defines acceptable standards of behaviour.			
There is the widest measure of agreement on these standards.			
There is fair and consistent application of these standards.			
Pupils contributed to the policy.			

The school provides curricular and other opportunities to encourage pupils to:			
take responsibility and show initiative;			
develop an understanding of living in a community.			

6

	Fully in place	Partly in place	Not in place

The school provides effectively for:			
personal and social education;			
health education;			
sex education;			
education on drug misuse.			

The curriculum inculcates respect, tolerance and good behaviour.			
The school provides a moral code as a basis for behaviour.			

The moral code is promoted throughout the life of the school.			

Overall evaluation:
On the scale of 0 – 10, where 0 = nothing yet in place, and 10 = everything in place, mark on the scale where you assess the school is at present with this aspect:

0	1	2	3	4	5	6	7	8	9	10

Is this aspect a priority for development?

If so, where on the scale would you like to be at the next review?

What action will achieve that?

(If prioritised, enter this aspect and identified action into the Development Plan.)

Aspect 3

The code of conduct – rules, rewards and sanctions

> **The behaviour policy should make clear the rules, rewards and sanctions that will promote the standards of behaviour the school wants to achieve.**

	Fully in place	Partly in place	Not in place

The behaviour policy includes:			
positive and constructive rules of conduct;			
the hierarchy of sanctions;			
a system of rewards for good behaviour;			
monitoring procedures to ensure consistency and fairness.			

Achievements are rewarded by positive recognition:			
of individual pupils;			
of classes or year groups;			
through mentions in assembly;			
certificates or prizes.			

Sanctions are applied:			
fairly and consistently to all pupils;			
taking account of all circumstances including the child's age;			
within a context of positive reinforcement of good behaviour;			
in proportion to offences.			

	Fully in place	Partly in place	Not in place

	Fully in place	Partly in place	Not in place
Punishments that are humiliating or degrading are never used.			
Punishments enable pupils to make reparation where appropriate.			

If detention is used as a sanction in school:			
it is in the behaviour policy;			
parents are given at least 24 hours notice in writing;			
it is only given by the head or a teacher authorised by the head;			
it is only used when reasonable, in terms of the punishment being proportionate;			
any special circumstances such as age, special needs, religious requirements and travel arrangements are taken into account.			

Overall evaluation:
On the scale of 0 – 10, where 0 = nothing yet in place, and 10 = everything in place, mark on the scale where you assess the school is at present with this aspect:

0	1	2	3	4	5	6	7	8	9	10

Is this aspect a priority for development?

If so, where on the scale would you like to be at the next review?

What action will achieve that?

(If prioritised, enter this aspect and identified action into the Development Plan.)

Aspect 4

Partnership with parents/carers

> The school should build a partnership with parents so they
> support the school in promoting good behaviour and attendance.

	Fully in place	Partly in place	Not in place
Parents and carers know the measures taken to promote good behaviour in school.			
The behaviour policy is brought to their attention at least once every school year.			

	Fully in place	Partly in place	Not in place
The governors have adopted a home-school agreement and an associated parental declaration.			
Parents were consulted on the home-school agreement.			

The home-school agreement specifies:			
the school's aims and values;			
the school's responsibilities;			
the parental responsibilities;			
the school's expectations of the pupils' conduct.			

The home-school agreement is clearly linked to school policies and practice, and is part of the whole school approach to partnership with parents.			

No child suffers any adverse consequences as a result of parents' failure or refusal to sign the home-school agreement e.g. refusal of a place at the school.			

	Fully in place	Partly in place	Not in place
Clear lines of communication with parents are established.			
Parents are encouraged to support good attendance and behaviour through home-school agreements, parents' meetings and newsletters.			
Relevant staff are made aware of adverse family circumstances sensitively.			
Family circumstances are taken into consideration when dealing with pupils.			
Staff involve parents early in problems with behaviour and action is agreed together.			

	Fully in place	Partly in place	Not in place
The school knows who has parental responsibility for all their pupils.			
There is a designated person for any children in public care in school.			

Overall evaluation:
On the scale of 0 – 10, where 0 = nothing yet in place, and 10 = everything in place, mark on the scale where you assess the school is at present with this aspect:

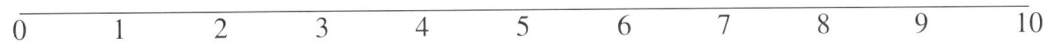

```
0     1     2     3     4     5     6     7     8     9     10
```

Is this aspect a priority for development?

If so, where on the scale would you like to be at the next review?

What action will achieve that?

(If prioritised, enter this aspect and identified action into the Development Plan.)

Aspect 5

Roles and responsibilities

> The governing body actively promotes the aims and principles that underpin the ethos of the school. The head teacher determines day-to-day policy and practice. Teachers work in ways that minimise disaffection. All staff provide good role models for pupils.

	Fully in place	Partly in place	Not in place

The governing body:			
has written a statement of general principles for the behaviour policy;			
has adopted a home-school agreement.			

The governing body and head teacher:			
have considered attendance policy;			
regularly monitor and review the anti-bullying, harassment and equal opportunity policies;			
inform the LEA annually of racist incidents.			

The head teacher has determined measures to promote good behaviour and to prevent all forms of bullying. These measures:			
are in the written behaviour policy;			
are made generally known;			
are brought to the attention of pupils, parents and all employed, or otherwise engaged to provide services, at the school, at least once a year.			

Arrangements for staff support are clear.			

	Fully in place	Partly in place	Not in place

Teachers:			
exercise authority clearly and fairly from the outset;			
hold the pupils' attention, involving them in the work and encouraging concentration and completion of the task;			
organise the work and grouping of pupils clearly and efficiently;			
support and control pupils, intervening according to need;			
establish mutual respect and proper habits of work;			
convey the importance of self-discipline and expectations of mature behaviour.			

All adults model values such as courtesy and respect with other adults and with pupils.			

Overall evaluation:

On the scale of 0 – 10, where 0 = nothing yet in place, and 10 = everything in place, mark on the scale where you assess the school is at present with this aspect:

0	1	2	3	4	5	6	7	8	9	10

Is this aspect a priority for development?

If so, where on the scale would you like to be at the next review?

What action will achieve that?

(If prioritised, enter this aspect and identified action into the Development Plan.)

Aspect 6

Anti-bullying and harassment

> **Measures should be in place to monitor and prevent all forms of bullying including racial and sexual harassment.**

	Fully in place	Partly in place	Not in place
There are policies in place with a view to eliminating bullying, including racial and sexual harassment.			

The governing body:			
has advised the head teacher of its views on specific measures to prevent bullying, and racial or sexual harassment;			
regularly reviews the anti-bullying and harassment policies;			
informs the LEA annually of the pattern and frequency of any racial incidents;			
monitors the impact of policies on different groups (by race, gender and disability).			

The head teacher has determined measures to prevent bullying.			
Prospectuses or other documents explain arrangements for reporting bullying and the action that will follow.			
Strategies cover break and playtimes.			

All staff:			
have received training;			
are alert to signs of bullying and act promptly and firmly;			
are aware of and consider vulnerable groups.			

	Fully in place	Partly in place	Not in place

	Fully in place	Partly in place	Not in place
Pupils are actively involved in preventive measures.			
All pupils are encouraged to report bullying.			

The racial harassment policy:			
makes explicit the school's intolerance of such behaviour;			
details how staff should deal with incidents;			
details how pupils should deal with incidents;			
states governors and parents are informed of incidents;			
suggests support is considered for pupils who have suffered racial harassment (at or outside school).			

All incidents and the action taken are recorded.			
All parents and pupils know the school's commitment to equal opportunities and the elimination of bullying and harassment.			

Overall evaluation:
On the scale of 0 – 10, where 0 = nothing yet in place, and 10 = everything in place, mark on the scale where you assess the school is at present with this aspect:

0	1	2	3	4	5	6	7	8	9	10

Is this aspect a priority for development?

If so, where on the scale would you like to be at the next review?

What action will achieve that?

(If prioritised, enter this aspect and identified action into the Development Plan.)

Aspect 7

Attendance

> Schools need to take a whole school approach to promote good attendance and to monitor any unauthorised absence so that prompt action can be taken.

	Fully in place	Partly in place	Not in place
A whole school approach to attendance and unauthorised absence has been considered by the governing body and the head teacher.			
A senior member of staff is responsible for attendance.			
Pupils causing concern are referred to the Education Welfare Service.			
The school supports any community-based action against truancy such as truancy watch schemes.			
IT is used to monitor attendance.			

Monitoring of attendance includes:			
unauthorised absence by race, by year group and by comparison with similar schools;			
unauthorised absence from individual lessons.			

Attendance is at or above the threshold of 95% in primary or 92% in secondary schools (or 90% in any year group).			

Pupils' good attendance is encouraged by:			
rewarding individual pupil, class or year group achievements in good attendance by mentions in assembly and awarding certificates;			
discussion between a pupil and the teacher responsible for the pupil's registration.			

	Fully in place	Partly in place	Not in place

Pupils' unauthorised absence is discouraged by:

	Fully in place	Partly in place	Not in place
passes confirming authority to be out of school;			
attendance checks, particularly for post-registration truancy.			

Parents are encouraged to support good attendance by:

	Fully in place	Partly in place	Not in place
first day contact for when pupils are absent;			
a clear procedure for reporting absence;			
the home-school agreement;			
newsletters and parents' meetings;			
reminding parents of school policy on holidays in term time;			

Overall evaluation:
On the scale of 0 – 10, where 0 = nothing yet in place, and 10 = everything in place, mark on the scale where you assess the school is at present with this aspect:

0	1	2	3	4	5	6	7	8	9	10

Is this aspect a priority for development?

If so, where on the scale would you like to be at the next review?

What action will achieve that?

(If prioritised, enter this aspect and identified action into the Development Plan.)

Aspect 8

Pupils at risk

> Children at risk of failing in school should be actively identified and strategies adopted, in collaboration with parents and other agencies where appropriate.

	Fully in place	Partly in place	Not in place
The progress of all pupils is regularly reviewed.			
Staff are aware of factors that put pupils at risk of failing in school and actively identify vulnerable pupils.			

	Fully in place	Partly in place	Not in place
(Secondary only)			
A check is made before the end of Year 9 to identify any pupils at risk of failure in school in partnership with the Careers Service, Education Welfare Officers and other agencies.			

	Fully in place	Partly in place	Not in place
A range of strategies are used for dealing with disruptive pupils, including:			
working with parents;			
sanctions;			
support units;			
mentoring;			
curricular flexibility.			

	Fully in place	Partly in place	Not in place
Specialist strategies, including involving other agencies, are used in cases involving drugs, harassment and crime.			

	Fully in place	Partly in place	Not in place
All pupils at risk of permanent exclusion have a Pastoral Support Programme (PSP) in place.			

	Fully in place	Partly in place	Not in place

Pastoral Support Programmes:

are overseen by a nominated member of staff;			
are short and practical, precise and realistic;			
are discussed and agreed with parents;			
are discussed and agreed with an LEA representative;			
involve other agencies as appropriate;			
are regularly reviewed with targets broken down into fortnightly tasks.			

Exclusion is only considered:

for serious breaches of behaviour policy;			
after a range of strategies have been tried;			
if other pupils are being put at serious risk.			
A PSP is used before any permanent exclusion.			

Overall evaluation:
On the scale of 0 – 10, where 0 = nothing yet in place, and 10 = everything in place, mark on the scale where you assess the school is at present with this aspect:

0	1	2	3	4	5	6	7	8	9	10

Is this aspect a priority for development?

If so, where on the scale would you like to be at the next review?

What action will achieve that?

(If prioritised, enter this aspect and identified action into the Development Plan.)

Aspect 9

SEN – emotional and behavioural difficulties

> Pupils with emotional and behavioural difficulties need approaches that are an extension of the whole school behaviour policy, working in partnership with parents, pupils and other agencies.

	Fully in place	Partly in place	Not in place

	Fully in place	Partly in place	Not in place
Behavioural needs are normally met within the context of the school's behaviour management policy.			
There are clear procedures so that staff actively identify pupils whose behaviour is causing concern.			
There is a graduated response with a wide array of strategies used to support pupils with behaviour difficulties.			

When *School Action* is required:			
all relevant information is collected;			
outside agencies working with pupils are contacted;			
parents are always consulted and kept informed of action and outcomes.			

The SENCO has clear procedures in place for:			
assessment;			
planning;			
monitoring;			
reviewing.			

Strategies employed are recorded on an IEP.			

	Fully in place	Partly in place	Not in place
The IEP is discussed with both the parent and the pupil.			
IEPs are delivered within the normal classroom setting.			

If *School Action Plus* is necessary:			
external support agencies are consulted;			
the plan is implemented at least in part and as far as possible, in the normal classroom setting.			

	Fully in place	Partly in place	Not in place
Pupils with EBD who are at risk of exclusion have a PSP or an IEP that fulfils the same criteria.			
The school manages to avoid excluding pupils with Statements, or who are part-way through the assessment process.			
The staff know that effective teaching skills for pupils with EBD are the same as those for all pupils.			

Overall evaluation:
On the scale of 0 – 10, where 0 = nothing yet in place, and 10 = everything in place, mark on the scale where you assess the school is at present with this aspect:

```
0      1      2      3      4      5      6      7      8      9      10
```

Is this aspect a priority for development?

If so, where on the scale would you like to be at the next review?

What action will achieve that?

(If prioritised, enter this aspect and identified action into the Development Plan.)

Aspect 10

The pupils' response

> The pupils respond to the school's policies and practice by demonstrating
> a high standard of behaviour that maximises their learning.

	Fully in place	Partly in place	Not in place

Pupils' attitudes to the school. Pupils:			
are keen and eager to come to school;			
show interest in school life and are involved in school activities.			

Pupils' behaviour. Pupils:			
behave well in lessons;			
behave well around the school;			
are courteous;			
are trustworthy;			
show respect for property.			

Personal development and relationships. Pupils:			
show initiative;			
are willing to take responsibility;			
form constructive relationships with one another;			
form constructive relationships with teachers and other adults;			
respect other people's differences, particularly their feelings, values and beliefs.			

	Fully in place	Partly in place	Not in place
reflect on what they do;			
understand the impact of their actions on others;			
work in an atmosphere free from oppressive behaviour such as bullying, sexism and racism.			

Attendance

	Fully in place	Partly in place	Not in place
Pupils have high levels of attendance.			
Pupils have low levels of unauthorised absence.			

There are no more than isolated incidents of:

	Fully in place	Partly in place	Not in place
disruptive, aggressive or intimidating behaviour;			
racist attitudes or sexist language or behaviour.			

	Fully in place	Partly in place	Not in place
Pupils' behaviour helps their learning rather than obstructs it.			
There is a high level of respect between pupils and teachers and other adults in the school.			

Overall evaluation:

On the scale of 0 – 10, where 0 = nothing yet in place, and 10 = everything in place, mark on the scale where you assess the school is at present with this aspect:

0   1   2   3   4   5   6   7   8   9   10

Is this aspect a priority for development?

If so, where on the scale would you like to be at the next review?

What action will achieve that?

(If prioritised, enter this aspect and identified action into the Development Plan.)

SCHOOL:

Behaviour Policy Development Plan

Date:

Aspect:	Action:	Responsibility:	Review: